ideals®
EASTER

Easter

Isabelle Carter Young

Unfolding of the lilies,
The singing of the birds
Tell of the joys of Easter
Better than we in words.

That peace and love triumphant
Over all the earth shall be—
This Resurrection message
Is brought to you and me.

IDEALS PUBLICATIONS
NASHVILLE, TENNESSEE

A Prayer in Spring
Robert Frost

Oh, give us pleasure in the flowers today;
And give us not to think so far away
As the uncertain harvest; keep us here
All simply in the springing of the year.

Oh, give us pleasure in the orchard white,
Like nothing else by day, like ghosts by night;
And make us happy in the happy bees,
The swarm dilating round the perfect trees.

And make us happy in the darting bird
That suddenly above the bees is heard,
The meteor that thrusts in with needle bill,
And off a blossom in mid-air stands still.

For this is love and nothing else is love,
The which it is reserved for God above
To sanctify to what far ends He will,
But which it only needs that we fulfill.

Photograph by Lefever/Grushow/
Grant Heilman Photography, Inc.

The Snowdrop

Hans Christian Andersen
Adapted by Carolyn T. Bailey

The snow lay deep, for it was wintertime. The winter winds blew cold, but there was one house where all was snug and warm. And in the house lay a little flower; in its bulb it lay, under the earth and the snow.

One day the rain fell and it trickled through the ice and snow down into the ground. And presently a sunbeam, pointed and slender, pierced down through the ground and tapped on the bulb.

"Come in," said the flower.

"I can't do that," said the sunbeam; "I'm not strong enough to lift the latch. I shall be stronger when the springtime comes."

"When will it come spring?" asked the flower of every little sunbeam that rapped on its door, but for a long time it was winter. The ground was still covered with snow, and every night there was ice in the water. The flower grew quite tired of waiting.

"How long it is!" it said. "I feel quite cramped; I must stretch myself and rise up a little. I must lift the latch, and look out, and say, 'Good morning' to the spring."

So the flower pushed and pushed. The walls were softened by the rain and warmed by the little sunbeams, so the flower shot up from under the snow, with a pale green bud on its stalk and some long, narrow leaves on either side. It was biting cold.

"You are a little too early," said the wind and the weather, but every sunbeam sang, "Welcome," and the flower raised its head from the snow, and unfolded itself—pure and white, and decked with green stripes. It was weather to freeze it to pieces—such a delicate little flower—but it was stronger than anyone knew. It stood in its white dress in the white snow, bowing its head when the snowflakes fell and raising it again to smile at the sunbeams. And every day it grew sweeter.

"Oh," shouted the children, as they ran into the garden, "see the snowdrop! There it stands so pretty, so beautiful—the first, the only one!"

Easter Song

Mary A. Lathbury

Snowdrops, lift your timid heads!
All the earth is waking;
Field and forest, brown and dead,
Into life are breaking.
Snowdrops, rise and tell the story:
How He rose, the Lord of glory.

Lilies! Lilies! Easter calls;
Rise to meet the dawning
Of the blessed light that falls
Through the Easter morning.
Ring your bells and tell the story:
How He rose, the Lord of glory.

Waken, sleeping butterflies;
Burst your narrow prison!
Spread your golden wings and rise,
For the Lord is risen.
Spread your wings and tell the story:
How He rose, the Lord of glory.

Snowdrops in spring snow. Photograph by Jane Grushow/Grant Heilman Photography, Inc.

Beyond
Hal Borland

Ever since that first Spring that ever was, man has stood at this season with awe in his eyes and wonder in his heart, seeing the magnificence of life returning and life renewed. And something deep within him has responded, whatever his religion or spiritual belief. It is as inevitable as sunrise that man should see the substance of faith and hope in the tangible world so obviously responding to forces beyond himself or his accumulated knowledge.

For all his learning and sophistication, man still instinctively reaches toward that force beyond, and thus approaches humility. Only arrogance can deny its existence, and the denial falters in the face of evidence on every hand. In every tuft of grass, in every bird, in every opening bud, there it is. We can reach so far with our explanations, and there still remains a force beyond, which touches not only the leaf, the seed, the opening petal, but man himself.

Spring is a result, not a cause. The cause lies beyond, still beyond, and it is the instinctive knowledge of this which inspires our festivals of faith and life and belief renewed. Resurrection is there for us to witness and participate in; but the resurrection around us still remains the symbol, not the ultimate truth; and men of goodwill instinctively reach for truth. Beyond the substance of Spring, of a greening and revivifying earth, of nesting and mating and birth, of life renewed. Thus we come to Easter and all the other festivals of faith, celebrating life and hope and the ultimate substance of belief, reaching like the leaf itself for something beyond, ever beyond.

Flowering crab apple trees along a stone wall in New Hampshire. Photograph by William H. Johnson

For, lo, the winter is past,
    the rain is over and gone;
the flowers appear on the earth;
the time of the singing
    of birds is come,
and the voice of the turtle
    is heard in our land.
—SONG OF SOLOMON 2:11–12

The Easter Joy

Margaret E. Sangster

The festival of Easter comes to us at a propitious time, "for lo, the winter is past; the rain is over and gone; the flowers appear on the earth, the time of the singing of birds is come; and the voice of the turtle is heard in our land" (Song of Solomon 2:11-12). Winter, with its rigor and cold, its ice and frost and inclement blasts, its tempests on land and sea, is an emblem of warfare; its silence and sternness ally it to grief. Spring comes dancing and fluttering in with flowers and music and the blithe step of childhood. Her signs are evident before she is really here herself. First come the bluebirds, harbingers of a host; a little later there will be wrens and robins and orioles, and all the troop which make the woods musical and build sociably around our country homes.

Then the flowers will come. Happy are they who shall watch their whole procession, from the pussywillow in March to the last blue gentian in October. We decorate our churches at Easter with the finest spoils of the hothouse— lilies, roses, palms, azaleas; nothing is too costly, nothing too lavish to be brought to the sanctuary or carried to the cemetery. Friend sends to friend the fragrant bouquet or the growing plant with the same tender significance which is evinced in the Christmas gifts, which carry from one heart to another a sweet message of love.

But God is giving us the Easter flowers in little hidden nooks in the forests, down by the corners of fences, in the sheltered places on the edges of the brook, and there we find the violet, the arbutus, and other delicate blossoms which lead the van for the great army of nature's efflorescence. The first flowers are more delicately tinted and of shyer look and more ephemeral fragrance than those which come later. They are the Easter flowers. Later on we shall have millions of blossoms and more birds than we can count: now in the garden and the field we have enough to remind us that "the winter is past, the rain is over and gone, the time of the singing of birds is come."

Rain lilies. Photograph by Dianne Dietrich Leis

In Time of Silver Rain

Langston Hughes

In time of silver rain
The earth
Puts forth new life again,
Green grasses grow
And flowers lift their
heads,
And over all the plain
The wonder spreads
Of life,
Of life,
Of life!

In time of silver rain
The butterflies
Lift silken wings
To catch a rainbow cry,
And trees put forth
New leaves to sing
In joy beneath the sky
As down the roadway
Passing boys and girls
Go singing too,
In time of silver rain
When spring
And life
Are new.

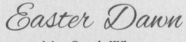

Easter Dawn

May Smith White

This is the pattern of the day I sought:
Soft rains to woo the early buds to flower,
With hope renewed as greater faith is wrought,
While sacred beauty fills the holy hour.

With ceasing rain to watch a new sun rise,
Shedding its brilliance with each golden ray—
Clouds rolling back, as true and nature-wise
As did the stone on that triumphant day.

And then to hear again God say to man:
"This is my hope and Resurrection plan."

Red tulips in the rain. Photograph by William H. Johnson

'Twas Easter Sunday. The full-blossomed trees filled all the air with fragrance and with joy.

—Henry Wadsworth Longfellow

The Little Trumpeters
Margaret Prescott Montague

I met the herald jonquils
    amid the grass today,
They trooped, the little trumpeters,
    in glad and green array;
Each held a golden bugle,
    and each a spear of green,
They said that they were messengers
    from April's misty queen.

Spring gave a swift direction,
    a hidden countersign—
Mayhap it was the bluebird's pipe—
    they straightened up in line;
There came a rushing whisper,
    a mystic sudden breeze;
It tossed their little horns on high,
    their trumpets to the trees.

They blew a golden message,
    a shout of love and spring,
A tiptoe blast of just one word—
    a word for stars to sing;
They tossed their living trumpets,
    the word they blew and blew—
And the word, O Lord of Life,
    the word was You! You! You!

*Daffodils skirting the trees. Photograph by
Larry Lefever/Grant Heilman Photography, Inc.*

Easter Lilies
Lona Pearson McDorman

A gardener took some shriveled bulbs
And planted them in rich, dark earth.
(They must remain there undisturbed
Until the time for their rebirth.)

All through the cheerless winter days,
They slept beneath the ice and snow.
The wise old gardener knew just when
The dormant bulbs would start to grow.

Spring sunshine came, and gentle showers;
Small shoots crept shyly through the ground;
Next, slender stocks, green leaves and buds;
And then one day the gardener found

A mass of bloom like radiant dawn!
When Easter bells rang sweet and clear,
The gardener cut his choicest flowers
And took them to the old church near.

He laid them on the chancel rail
Then reverently bowed his head.
"Dear Lord, here is my gift
    for Thee:
Rare beauty born of what
    seemed dead."

In the Garden
C. Austin Miles

I come to the garden alone,
While the dew is still on the roses,
And the voice I hear,
Falling on my ear,
The Son of God discloses.

And He walks with me,
    and He talks with me,
And He tells me I am His own;
And the joy we share as we tarry there,
None other has ever known.

He speaks, and the sound of His voice
Is so sweet the birds hush their singing,
And the melody
That He gave to me,
Within my heart is ringing.

And He walks with me,
    and He talks with me,
And He tells me I am His own;
And the joy we share as we tarry there,
None other has ever known.

I'd stay in the garden with Him
Though the night around me be falling,
But He bids me go;
Thro' the voice of woe
His voice to me is calling.

And He walks with me,
    and He talks with me,
And He tells me I am His own;
And the joy we share as we tarry there,
None other has ever known.

*Tulips and daffodils in West Shores Acres Display Garden in
Mt. Vernon, Washington. Photograph by Dianne Dietrich Leis*

Why Bother to Have a Garden?

Wanda M. Read

Why do we bother with gardens, when good, fresh produce is always "in season"—and a bargain as well—at the supermarket? Why do we enslave ourselves, driven by the season and the need to get the ground tilled, then to plant, and finally to haul in the harvest in quantities determined by the garden and not by our own wishes?

We work to save our garden from sure death when rain is scarce, and to save it from strangulation when rain and weeds are ample. Then we endure steamy hours in the kitchen, canning and freezing, pickling and jelling, putting up the harvest, when it would be far more pleasant to be outdoors.

Why do we garden? Because it feels good to us. Gardening felt especially good to my husband and me after a year of drought, when our tiller dug deep, but turned up only dust and the soil lay fallow all summer long. Late rains were wasted, nurturing only a feeble stand of weeds to haunt us.

Gardening feels good now, after such a dry, fallow year. We planted early and watched for any signs of thirst. We mulched heavily, both to conserve precious moisture and to help hold our ground against the inevitable offspring of the previous year's weed cover.

Each garden is a new creation. We work it out on graph paper, flowers in each plot, double cropping, companion planting, always with an eye to height, to afternoon shade, and to morning sun. Always, however, nature has the final say in what grows where, how much of it grows, and when it matures; beauty balances utility. Convenience of harvest would be nice, but usually everything comes at once, just as it always has.

Working in our garden, we stop to look out beyond our plots, to the grain fields around us and the woods beyond them.

"It's all ours," I comment. As far as we can see, as far as we can imagine, these are our foothills. No matter that we do not pay taxes on all of it or hold a deed to it. It is ours this day.

As we listen, we find that we are not alone. Robins bounce from cherry tree to grape arbor, bees zoom between cosmos and bean blossoms, each seeming to be tending a garden of his own. Near my resting feet, an ant hauls a tiny stick over blades of grass and a small black beetle works at a clump of earth. As we go back to work, we are filled with new inspiration.

"We have made a good garden here," I say as I pinch suckers from a burgeoning tomato plant.

"Not us. We only planted it," my husband reminds me as he winds the lengthening tendrils of a stalk of Blue Lake beans around a newly set pole.

This is why we garden. It is a cooperative system. We work, we listen, we take direction; we share in the harvest.

"We assisted, then, in making a good garden here," he agrees. We don't make a garden, and we don't simply take from its store. We are privileged, rather, to have a role in the process.

Photograph by Jessie Walker

Easter
Author Unknown

Easter is here and blossom time; the music of young leaves, the unheard melodies of daisies in the grass where the footsteps of spring have found a resting place!

It seems so short a while since we gazed from our windows at the bare, sodden earth, where the small brown bulbs were still asleep, waiting . . . waiting . . .

It seems but yesterday that we discovered the first snowdrop, and the new-found sun fell all across the garden like a sudden benediction.

During the last month we have caught the first notes of that wild music which has been gathering through the dark days of winter, and now the garden is full of sweet singing. Each blade of grass, each tiny drop of dew, holds a note of music; with the winter past, and the summer all before, even the rain has the sound of a song.

Today the great miracle of spring—old as the hills yet ever new—comes with a rush of joy to gladden the heart of the world.

Soft, pink bud and every young and happy thing: we add it to our prayers that this rare loveliness may linger long for our delight.

Song and scent and blossom time: the Easter Resurrection is complete.

Horned violets. Photograph by Alan and Linda Detrick/Grant Heilman Photography, Inc.

Easter in the Woods

Frances Frost

This dawn when the mountain cherry lifts
Its frail white bloom among dark pines,
And chipmunks flash small happy paws
Along old tumbled boundary lines,
This golden morning when the vixen
Nuzzles her five young foxes forth
To roll in ferns in the Easter sun,
Again the woods know soft green birth.

Snuffed by a puffball infant rabbit
Are yellow violets by the spring;
Among half-opened apple buds
A wood thrush tilts its head to sing.
Risen is He! And they are His
Who scamper under warm blue skies,
Who nibble little fists of grass,
And gaze on the earth with glad eyes.

Loveliest of Trees

A. E. Housman

Loveliest of trees, the cherry now
Is hung with bloom along the bough,
And stands about the woodland ride
Wearing white for Eastertide.

Now, of my threescore years and ten,
Twenty will not come again,
And take from seventy springs a score,
It only leaves me fifty more.

And since to look at things in bloom
Fifty springs are little room,
About the woodlands I will go
To see the cherry hung with snow.

*Flowering cherry tree with daffodils and tulips
in Monroe, Oregon. Photograph by Dennis Frates*

The Legend of the Dogwood

Author Unknown

At the Creation, God made the dogwood tree tall and strong, equal to the mighty oaks which grew alongside it. The dogwood was a proud tree—it raised its head above the others in the forest—and its wood was world-renowned and used to build strong ships, magnificent palaces, and great bridges. So strong and firm was the dogwood's wood, in fact, that the Romans used it as the timbers for the crosses on which they crucified criminals.

When the Lord was sentenced to death, a dogwood was chosen for His cross. The tree became so distressed that its mighty limbs quivered and its leaves shed in mourning. So deep was the dogwood's sorrow that Jesus took pity on it and made a promise:

"Because of your compassion for me, mighty dogwood, never again shall your kind grow large enough to be used for a cross. Henceforth your trunk shall be slender, your branches bent and twisted.

"Each spring your blossoms will form the shape of a cross with two long and two short petals. They shall be as pure in color as ivory, but on the outer edge of each petal there will be the stains of my blood. The center of your flowers will be a crown of thorns—so that all who see it will remember it was upon a dogwood tree that I was crucified, and this tree shall not be mutilated nor destroyed but cherished and protected as a reminder of my agony and death upon the cross."

Now, the dogwood blossoms serve each spring as a beautiful and poignant reminder of the glorious Resurrection of our Lord Jesus Christ.

Dogwood tree in bloom. Photograph by
Rob Nunnington/Oxford Scientific/Jupiter Images

Resurrection
Earle J. Grant

Lord, I cannot doubt
The Resurrection
When spring is here,
And I witness the sight
Of bare apple trees
Miraculously turned
Into bridal bouquets
Of lovely white.
For I know that this
Transcendant power—
That could only come
From One Divine,
Which brings to life
Somnolent apple tress—
Will, one day, resurrect
This body of mine.

Always Easter
Grace V. Watkins

You say it happened long ago
And in a far-off land
Where men and women spoke a tongue
I would not understand,
That centuries have come and gone
Since that triumphant day,
And that the garden where He walked
Is half a world away.

He walks in every garden, friend;
And every rock-sealed tomb
Opens 'neath His shining hand
As springtime flowers bloom.
For every dawn is Easter dawn:
On every sunrise hill
The earthbound glimpse eternity
And meet the Master still.

Easter 101

Pamela Kennedy

Teaching first and second graders in Sunday School is an inspiring, if sometimes daunting, proposition. A child of six or seven years has that dangerous mix of knowledge, experience, and spontaneity that brings unexpected interpretations to the most ordinary situations. When confronted with the great events and teachings of Scripture, these little believers often bring fresh insights that give new life to even the mustiest passages.

I recall teaching a lesson on the Creation to a group of children one morning. After explaining how God spoke the different elements of the universe into existence, one particularly impressed little fellow raised his hand and asked, "No lasers, no magic words, no nothing?" I said he had pretty well summed up the whole situation. "Wow," he added. "That beats Superman!"

When my own son came home from his class one Sunday, carrying a crayon drawing of two men and a dog warming themselves by a fire, I asked him about the day's lesson.

"Well," he replied, pointing to the figures in the picture, "these are those guys at the fiery furnace."

"Weren't there three guys?" I questioned, recalling Shadrach, Meshach, and Abednego, thrown into the fire by an angry Persian king.

"No, Mom," he patiently explained. "There was Shadrach and Meshach, and a pet named Go!"

Although I often had doubts about the amount of real theology dispensed in my class, one Easter I was given a lesson I'll never forget.

Searching for a way to make the different elements of the Easter story real to my young students, I decided to allow them to take part in the preparation of the lesson. On Palm Sunday, I gave each child a hollow plastic egg. "Next week," I said, "I want each of you to bring back your egg with something inside that reminds you of Easter; then we will talk about all the things we have brought in to share."

The class was an interesting mix of youngsters. We had quiet and vocal ones, rambunctious ones, and those who preferred to sit and draw pictures quietly. But my biggest challenge that year was a little boy named Marty. Marty had satiny black hair and big brown eyes that darted around the room as if he were expecting to see something frightening any minute. He often refused to take part in activities and his papers were rarely completed. But the thing that bothered me most about Marty was that he hardly ever spoke. It was difficult to gauge his understanding, and I was convinced he was getting nothing out of Sunday School class although he was there most Sundays. His mother assured me, "Marty loves Sunday School." But I figured she was just being polite.

After I handed out the plastic eggs, I showed the children how they came apart in the middle and repeated the instructions. "Does everyone understand?" I asked. Little heads nodded back at me. "Marty?" I inquired. Startled, the brown eyes raised, then lowered quickly. He nodded slowly as he pushed the halves of his egg back together. I sighed as the children left that day and wondered what I could do to reach little Marty with God's love.

On Easter Sunday, the children tumbled into the classroom, resplendent in ruffles and floral

First Congregational Church in Haverhill, New Hampshire. Photograph by William H. Johnson

prints, miniature suits and clip-on ties. They eagerly placed their colored plastic eggs in the basket I had positioned in the story circle. I was glad to see Marty drop his egg in with the others and wondered what he had brought to share.

After a few minutes of welcome activities, we moved to the chairs grouped around the basket. One by one the children came to open their eggs and share their symbols of Easter. One girl brought a tiny chick made of yarn; another brought a candy egg. Thomas, my class clown, produced a coiled-up pipe cleaner and informed us, "It's because Easter is in the SPRING! Get it?" He collapsed on the floor, laughing hysterically at his own wit.

Having recovered from Thomas's offering, we continued around the group. It seemed that most of the children had forgotten about the religious significance of the holiday, and I was feeling like a failure as a teacher until Sarah produced a little metal cross and we were able to get into the more spiritual side of things.

Finally, there was one egg left and I looked at Marty. "Would you like to open your egg for us, Marty?" He shook his head.

"How about if I open it for you? I'm sure everyone is looking forward to seeing what you brought." He looked up at me shyly and gave a little nod.

Carefully, I pulled apart the blue egg. Nothing fell out. I tipped the halves and peered in. There was nothing stuck inside.

"Marty didn't bring nothin'!" observed one of the boys. Some of the others giggled.

My mind was racing. How could I spare this sensitive child the embarrassment he was obviously experiencing? "Marty, is there something you'd like to share about your egg?" I asked, grasping at a possible way out.

Tentatively, Marty got out of his chair and came to my side. He took the two halves of the blue plastic egg and then walked over to the big picture in the center of our bulletin board. In a small, but clear voice, he said to the children:

"I *didn't* bring nothin'. I brought Easter."

My eyes filled with tears as I saw the truth Marty alone had understood; for over his head on the bulletin board was a picture of the empty tomb.

Memory
Shirley Sallay

Eastertime means Easter eggs of rainbow-colored hue;
A soft and cuddly bunny and a jelly bean or two;

A brand-new Easter bonnet on top of baby's head;
A bit of artificial grass in green or gold or red;

A little woven basket beside each bedroom door,
Where children may discover them
     at dawn, as they explore.

Just a bit of whimsy
     for a special holiday . . .
Moments shared together,
     then gently tucked away.

Things Like This
Shirley Sallay

She had one of my aprons tied up around her chin,
Its vivid red contrasted with the ivory of her skin.
The hard-boiled eggs were ready, so were the vivid dyes,
And excitement was reflected in the glimmer of her eyes.

She chose one of the eggs and dipped it in the brew;
She turned it and submerged it for just a moment or two.
I wondered as I watched her, if she spun a childhood dream
Into the swirls of color; for they seemed to have a theme.

Perhaps she thought of ribbons or a rainbow which did stray
Or maybe of the sunset we see at end of day.
They might be flower petals or the crystals seen in frost;
She doesn't have to tell me. (I'd not ask at any cost.)

For, you see, a girl needs secrets to think about and treasure;
'Tis things like coloring Easter eggs that happy childhoods measure.

Colored eggs next to an azalea bush.
Photograph by Dianne Dietrich Leis

A Country-Style Easter

Darlene Kronschnabel

Easter was like no other time in Mother's country kitchen. It was a holy day, and held an exciting freshness, a born-again feeling unique to this holiday.

Since Mother held to many of her mother's European food customs while adding some of her own, Easter was filled with special foods. Aside from a regular menu, special breads, colored eggs, and ham were always on her Easter menu.

Our favorite Easter kitchen tradition centered on ham—preferably home-cured and hickory-smoked in Father's smokehouse—and at least six dozen eggs. Sometimes Mother used eight dozen. She boiled the hickory-smoked ham for at least an hour in a 20-quart kettle, then let it cool in the liquid. While it cooled, we washed the eggs and let them warm to room temperature.

After the ham cooled, she removed it from the liquid and carefully added the eggs to the ham broth. The ham liquid and eggs were returned to the heat and kept at a low boil for about a half hour. She then let the eggs cool in the ham broth.

"This is important," she stressed, "to draw in the ham's smoky flavor."

Some claimed they couldn't taste any hint of ham in the hard-boiled eggs. However, if you ate one plain boiled and then one of Mom's Easter eggs, you noticed the delightful difference. We enjoyed the ham-flavored eggs so much we nibbled and snacked on them between meals rather than eating candy.

While she tended the boiling eggs, Mother repeated age-old egg-related legends and myths she'd heard, I'm sure, from her own mother.

"Some say," she began, "if you find two yolks in an Easter egg, that is a sign of coming financial prosperity. If you refuse an Easter egg you endanger your friendship with the person offering it."

"And," she went on, "Easter eggs cooked on Good Friday will promote fertility of trees and crops and protect against a sudden death."

"In some parts of Europe," she continued, "it's a legend that eggs laid on Good Friday, if kept for a hundred years, will have their yolks turn to diamonds."

When I laughed at the idea of eggs turning to diamonds, she scolded me. "Eggs are the symbol of spring fertility and new life. They deserve respect."

Between boiling the ham and eggs (which usually took up most of the day) and baking an assortment of special breads, the kitchen filled with rich, tantalizing aromas that teased and taunted us all day long into begging for just a taste to supplement our meager meals. (A strict traditionalist, Mother insisted that the Lenten fasting continue until Easter Sunday morning.)

At last, Easter Sunday morning arrived. After we'd found our candy-filled baskets, the plates of braided egg bread rings and bunny rolls on the breakfast table next to the platters of ham and ham-flavored eggs made all the waiting worthwhile.

Photograph by Nancy Matthews

Easter 1912

Catherine Otten

When I was a child, I lived in a house that was divided into a home and a store. My favorite place in the store was the candy corner. The west front window and a glass counter next to it was given over completely to displaying candy. The candy corner ushered in all holidays of the year.

Next to Christmas, my favorite holiday was Easter, and our candy corner helped to make it so. The candy window was full of pink and white and chocolate marshmallow rabbits and eggs. Soft yellow, sugary chicks lay in neat rows between the solid milk chocolate rabbits, elegant in their shiny gold and silver foil wrappers. Tiny tin frying pans containing creamy, candy sunny-side-up fried eggs and other Easter novelties, all at a penny each, added to the charm of the display.

The shiny glass candy counter attracted the older customers. Pretty dishes of pastel bonbons, maple and chocolate fudge, coated nuts, caramels, and chocolate creams—all selling for a penny a piece—made a mouthwatering display. Tall jars of jelly beans and stick candy decorated the back shelves of the candy corner along with the fancy be-ribboned boxes of gift candy.

Because there were so many sweets around to tempt young appetites, we children were allowed only small amounts occasionally. However, both my little sister and I had a "sweet box" which held many forbidden goodies to munch when we were playing up in our room—away from the grownups. This "sweet box" was always hidden in the farthest corner of our closet.

"What's all this?" demanded Mama one day as she cleaned the shelves in the children's closet.

"It's my sweet box," I confessed, grabbing my treasure off the trash heap.

"Throw it out," Mama ordered mercilessly. "We'll have bugs and moths all over the place. The closet is no place for food, especially for sweet, sticky stuff like this!"

We should have known better than to try to hide anything those days before Easter. Our house was always thoroughly scrubbed and cleaned to make ready for the holiday. Nothing was safe from broom and scrub brush and Mama's eagle eye. She always seemed to know when we got into mischief, even when her back was turned.

"Alleluia, alleluia! Let the loud hosannas ring!" Those hosannas were loud and thrilling even at daybreak on very cold Easter mornings. Our Easter always started with a sunrise service. The long, cold trek home was full of happy anticipation; for the Easter basket hunt began the minute we got home. I shall never forget the year that Toby, our shaggy shepherd dog, found our baskets first. He must have begun his hunt as soon as we left for the service that morning. Even our disappointment

Candy display at the General Store Museum, Cedarburg, Wisconsin. Photograph by age fotostock/SuperStock

couldn't cover up the amusing sight Toby made lying guiltily and quietly in the middle of the mess he had made of all those lovely Easter nests.

Breakfast on Easter morning was a meal to remember. Usually, some of our cousins, aunts, and uncles came home with us. The Easter hunt went on while Mama was busy frying sausages and scrambling eggs. The table was full of baked goodies Mama had made the day before. As we all joined hands at the table, Papa led the grace asking God's blessing and a fervent wish for everyone's health and happiness, and this day, instead of the usual "Amen," we all shouted "Alleluia!"

The Plum Silk Dress

Blanche Floyd

Isn't it pretty? You'll like the color," Mama assured me. And I did. My new Sunday dress was the smooth, bright color of plum jam, just perfect with my dark brown hair and eyes. As usual, I tried to pretend that the big brown freckles were really not there.

I was seven years old, one of eight children in a Methodist preacher's family. Getting a new dress was really an occasion in those days. Proudly, I hung my dress in the closet along with my sister's clothes and my own meager wardrobe. I lovingly smoothed the shiny pleats and folds.

Sunday morning finally came and we were off to church, brushed and polished and dressed in our best. It was a cool day, but I needed no coat. My new dress would keep me warm.

After church, we were invited to the Warrens' house to eat a huge Sunday dinner and visit awhile. They had lots of children and we loved visiting them. The younger children were allowed to sit on the porch after we ate and play quiet guessing games. We knew not to play rowdy games on Sunday, or to mess up our church clothes.

Tiring of quiet games, we moved away from the house to walk down to the creek. We stayed away from the joggling board set under the great oak trees. As much as we all loved to bounce on the board, we knew that we should not have that much fun on the Sabbath Day.

A low fence edged the yard to keep small children near the house and the cattle near the creek. The boys took the fence in one leap, but the girls walked sedately to the gate. Not me. Once the girls had turned their backs, the old tomboy in me took over and I went sailing over the fence after the boys—almost!

At the sound of cloth ripping, my first thought was of my new dress. My beautiful plum silk dress had caught a snag on the fence. There was a long tear down the side. I stumbled over to a log and sank down to inspect the damage. The tear was longer and worse that I had thought. What could I do?

When the parents called, we rushed back to the house and then to the car for our trip home. I pulled off my dress as soon as we got home and hung it carefully so the tear wouldn't show—my sister might tell if she saw it.

After our supper of milk, cake, and fruit, we all got ready to walk over to the church again. I knew I would be expected to wear my new dress, so I put it on, lapping the tear over and pinning it. It was warmer than ever, but I put on my coat and buttoned it up. Then I brushed my hair, ignored my freckles, and went out with the brothers and sisters.

During the service, the church got warmer and I began to sweat. Mama motioned to me to take off my coat. I shook my head, but I decided to unbutton the top button. As I settled down, the pin stuck in my leg and I bounced straight up. Mama looked my way and I eased down again.

So there I sat, sweating to death in my buttoned-up coat and bleeding to death from a pin scratch, with my lovely dress ruined. Daddy was saying from the pulpit, "Lift up your hearts! Be happy in God's beautiful world!" My misery increased.

School, play, and chores took up my time during the next week, so I almost forgot about the dress. When I did remember it, I would screw up my eyes tight and whisper, "Please, God, don't let Mama find out I tore my new dress!"

Sunday dawned bright and fair and warm. What to wear? I looked at my old Sunday dress, inches too short. Could I bear to wear my coat again all day over my torn dress?

Reluctantly, I took down my plum silk dress and slipped it on. I reached for the rip, expecting to feel the pin again. But where was it? Gingerly I felt and looked for the long, ugly tear. It was gone. Had the whole thing been a nightmare? Was it a miracle?

I looked down at the skirt. The pleats swung evenly in place and the dress was freshly pressed. From the door I heard Mama say, "Are you ready to go?" She was smiling at me.

And then I knew. Mama had fixed my beautiful dress so the tear didn't show. I flew to the door and wrapped my arms around her waist. "Thank you, Mama," I whispered.

She dropped a kiss on the top of my head and down the hall we went, gathering brothers and sisters along the way.

"I don't think I need my coat today," I sang, until the others made me hush.

Photograph by Larry Lefever/
Grant Heilman Photography, Inc.

Easter Hat

Esta McElrath

A little girl with freckled nose,
Curly hair, cheeks like a rose,
Wore a hat with upturned brim,
Morning glories, and ribbon trim.

She went to church on Easter Day;
Her feet were light, her heart was gay.
She walked along with buoyant tread
As down the aisle the usher led.

A look of joy upon her face,
Within the pew she took her place.
All eyes were turned with knowing smiles
To see a girl so smart in style.

Her Easter Bonnet

Lola M. Hazard

Standing before a mirror,
Turning this way and that,
Admiringly she views herself
And her new Easter hat.

Rosebuds tucked around the brim,
Bits of ribbon and lace,
A milliner's art in miniature
As it frames her little face.

A beautiful Easter bonnet
Gives a feminine heart a thrill,
Whether she's eight or eighty,
And I think it always will.

Photograph by Jessie Walker

On Easter Morning
Kathryn Stephenson Wilhelm

Tulips marching, two by two,
On stately stems in brilliant hue.

Children marching, two by four,
Marching through the front church door,
Dressed in tulips' brilliant hues
To brighten somber, stately pews.

Eastertime Parade
Hilda Butler Farr

In a yellow coat and bonnet
Our miss will be arrayed,
A charming new addition
To the Eastertime parade.

Of course she'll not be walking;
She hasn't reached that stage,
But she'll be competition
For girls of any age.

So in a yellow bonnet
And coat her Mommy made,
She'll be a baby model
In the Eastertime parade.

Photograph by Lefever/Grushow/
Grant Heilman Photography, Inc.

The Little Town Church

Loise Pinkerton Fritz

Springtime has come to the little town church,
The little town church of white.
The spreading, lone forsythia
Is covered with florets bright—

Beautiful florets of yellowish gold
That brighten the still-dull earth.
Springtime has come in a colorful dress,
And come to this small-town church.

Easter has come to the little town church,
The little town church I know.
The choir is singing, "Christ's risen today,"
While bells chime sounds of hope.

Easter has come to the little town church,
To churches in cities and dells.
And the Christ of Easter shall come and dwell
In the hearts of the people, as well.

Christ Church, St. Simons Island, Georgia.
Photograph by William H. Johnson

An Easter to Remember

Verla A. Mooth

In the Ozarks of southwestern Missouri, my small hometown did not have a church in which to worship, but we gathered in the schoolhouse each Sunday for Sunday school and preaching. If there was no preacher, we sang hymns and shared testimonies.

From the time I was a small child, I had been asked to sing in the choir. I often sang solos, and I participated in all the special programs.

Although Easter Sunday was always observed in a special way, the spring of 1933 was something different. A few years earlier, some in the community had attended an Easter sunrise service in a city park twenty miles away. It was often mentioned as being the most inspirational service they had ever attended.

As Easter drew near, someone suggested that we hold our own sunrise service. Grandpa George suggested we could use his cow pasture down the hollow from where we lived. It was a nice, wide hollow with steep hills on each side. The grazing cows had kept the grass and weeds eaten so low it was almost like a mowed lawn. He said he would move the cows to another pasture. Those who had trucks and cars could park them at his house and walk down to the hollow. The service was set for six AM. Everyone was excited about planning our own sunrise service, but no one was more excited than I was. I had been asked to sing the closing song, "Christ Arose."

Mama had been saving her egg money to buy material to make me a new dress for Easter. Mama always tried to help me have more confidence in myself by telling me that I was just as pretty as my sister was. My sister was four years older than I, and all my life I had lived in her shadow. She had dark brown hair and lovely hazel eyes and had developed into a young woman at an early age.

I was tall and skinny and had blue eyes and light brown hair. Many times those blue eyes filled with tears when I overheard some thoughtless person comparing me to my sister. "Verla is smart and she can sing and recite as good as anyone, but she is so plain, while her sister is so good-looking!"

Mama would comfort me by saying, "Pretty is as pretty does." I assumed she meant that I was "pretty does."

Mama had seen a picture of a lovely dress in the catalog. She bought pale yellow voile and cut out a sleeveless dress and a short jacket with several rows of gathered ruffles that made the jacket look like the petals on a flower. It was the most beautiful, grown-up fashion I had ever had. Mama told me how lovely I looked, but I still had doubts.

Easter Sunday, we awoke to a cold, drizzling rain. The sky was dark and overcast. Mama started to get out the winter coats. Spring coats were a luxury we couldn't afford. When Mama handed me mine, I laid it on a chair and said, "Mama, I will not wear that old, worn-out coat. I want to show my beautiful new dress." Mama tried to convince me that I would freeze and catch my death of cold, but I was determined.

We hadn't walked any distance down the hollow before I was shivering, but I didn't mention it. I walked along with my head down to keep my face warm, oblivious to my surroundings.

We arrived at the place the service was to be

held just as friends and neighbors began to gather. It had been decided that the singers would stand on the hillside. Everyone huddled together to keep warm. Although the choir tried to put feeling into their words, our teeth chattered.

We had secured a preacher for the special event. He put deep feeling into his message of the Resurrection and spirits began to lift. A few loud "Amens!" could be heard from the crowd.

I forgot about being cold and listened intently. Soon it

was time for my solo. Just as I stepped out a few feet from the others and started the first line of my song, "Low in a grave He lay," the clouds parted and a glorious burst of sunlight rose above the hillside, flooding the hollow with warming rays of light. The bright beams of sun hit me squarely in my face, casting a radiant glow on my yellow dress.

I felt warm all over! The words of the song, "He arose, He arose," sounded against the other side of the hill and echoed back through the valley below. I suddenly realized that the ground beneath my feet was covered with beautiful spring violets and wood daisies.

The service was over. Comments about how beautiful the sunrise service was and how we should do it again each year could be heard through the crowd.

On the way home, Mama put her arm around me as we walked along and said, "Honey, I was so

proud of you. The sun shining upon your face as you sang made you look just like a beautiful spring flower bursting into bloom."

I whispered back in an awed voice, "It is all right, Mama. I think I now understand what Easter is all about." And it was true. Never again would I compare myself with anyone else. I was God's beautiful creation in my own right. As we left the meadowlands and entered a wood, I saw that all of the dogwood, redbud, and wild cherry trees were in full bloom, each different but beautiful in its own way.

It was at that moment that the final wrapping of the shroud of self-doubt which had bound me for fourteen years was laid aside. On that unforgettable Easter Sunday morning almost sixty-five years ago, my spirit burst forth in songs of praise, harmonizing with the birds who were singing their own songs of Easter praise to the Creator.

Nature's Easter Music

Lucy Larcom

The flowers from the earth have arisen;
They are singing their Easter song.
Up the valleys and over the hillsides
They come, an unnumbered throng.

Oh listen! The wildflowers are singing
Their beautiful songs without words!
They are pouring the soul of their music
Through the voices of happy birds.

Every flower to a bird has confided
The joy of its blossoming birth—

The wonder of its resurrection
From its grave in the frozen earth.

The buttercup's thanks for the sunshine
The goldfinch's twitter reveals;
And the violet trills through the bluebird,
Of the heaven that within her she feels.

The song sparrow's exquisite warble
Is born in the heart of the rose—
Of the wild rose, shut in its calyx,
Afraid of belated snows.

Photograph by Nancy Matthews

Song of Easter

Celia Thaxter

Easter lilies! Can you hear
What they whisper, low and clear?

In dewy fragrance they unfold
Their splendor sweet, their snow and gold.

Every beauty-breathing bell
News of heaven has to tell.

Listen to their mystic voice;
Hear, O mortal, and rejoice!

Hark, their soft and heavenly chime!
Christ is risen for all time!

Art and blue heaven,
April and God's larks,
Green reeds and
Sky-scattering river.
A stately music—
Enter, God!

—ROBERT LOUIS STEVENSON

The Awakening

Jan Stephens

The pink fingers of dawn slip over the gray edge of morning, giving hint that a golden-haired sun will soon peer over the treetops to steal a glimpse of a sleepy world. This intrusion is announced by the chirping call of quail as the covey breaks their nocturnal circle to begin feeding. Cottontails, with bellies full from a night of foraging, hurridly steal one last bite of the dew-laden greenery as they streak away to underground tunnels.

In the midst of a cluster of green ribbon leaves, the tip of a slender spear moves from the darkness of a subterranean existence heavenward, as if in an unannounced race with the rising sun to the apex of the sky.

The tip of the shaft is a pale green spearhead whose erectness stands in contrast to dark green leaves, bowed submissively at its base, as if they know some secret of the miracle to come.

Minutes of the morning fall like droplets from an icicle on a warming winter day as the spearhead begins a gradual swell, and pale green transforms to ivory.

Drops of time continue as rising air thermals bring turkey vultures spiraling skyward, and the spearhead's swelling increases as if some underground source is sending thermals through the shaft from below.

Red-tailed hawks join the air currents as the enlarged ellipsoid of milk-white segments begins to separate along the lines of indentation. The sun, now well over the horizon, continues its rise to observe this wonder taking place in its domain. For what kind of monarch would let some miracle happen unawares?

Above the humble ribboned leaves, ivory petal-segments swell from the center and begin a graceful backward arch.

So slowly they bend that their movement seems halted to all save those of the same kind who mark their progress in millimeters of beauty.

The white petals lay back, exposing pollen-dipped stamens that lure insects for a closer look at its golden treasure.

The sun now stands at the peak of the heavens in admiration of the awakening; the lily stands at the vertex of its beauty. Tied in the race, but both victors in their own realm, they recall the victory of another awakening so long ago.

Trumpet lily. Photograph by Larry Lefever/
Grant Heilman Photography, Inc.

Dawn Anthems
Ruth Powell Singer

In my garden this morning
Beauty reigned supreme;
I saw each chaliced lily
Waken from her dream.

The dew had washed their faces;
They sparkled with delight.

Their gowns shimmered with stardust,
Left over from last night.

Dawn was robed in rose and gold,
And I heard the woodbirds sing
Anthems of adoration
To Christ the risen King.

First Light
Rose Terry Cook

With the first bright, slant beam,
Out of the chilling stream
Their cups of fragrant light
Golden and milky white
From folded darkness spring,
To hail their King.

Consider these, my soul!
How the blind buds unroll
Touched with one tranquil ray
Of rising day,
Into the full delight
Of lilies white.

Out of thy streaming tears,
Thy chill and darkening fears,
Oh, sleeping soul, awake!
Lo, on thy lonely lake,
Thy sun begins to shine,
Thy Light and Life divine!

Consider these, my heart!
Dreaming and cold thou art:
Swift from thyself up-spring,
Shine for thy King.
Rise in His light,
With garments white,
Forget the night:
The Lord hath arisen.

Olin Criswell lilies and wild muskmallow.
Photograph by William H. Johnson

Easter Sunrise
Rachel Van Creme

The black of night begins to break—
Deep purple shadows in its wake;
A golden fringe outlines the hills;
Into the valley it slowly spills.
The clouds are shot with shafts of gold
And banked in beauty to behold;
The highest hills are rimmed with fires—
Cathedrals, lifting holy spires.

The doubts of night dissolve away
Before the dawning of the day;
Our hearts rejoice in grateful prayer
Before His holy altar, there.
And voices lifting free and high
Salute the sunrise in the sky.

Easter Bells
Mamie Ozburn Odum

The night was still before the dawn,
Mystic shadows were softly drawn.
Then came an echoed wave of sound
Encompassing the world around,
And in each heart the music swells
The calling voice of Easter bells.

The sweet tone clings and softly peals;
In reverence the whole world kneels,
The small, the large, the weak, the strong.
Each heart is filled with Easter song
And haste to worship at the swells
Of the golden tones of Easter bells.

And in the roseate golden east
We seek and find a holy tryst.
Here love of God is sought and found,
The grave is naught but garden ground.
And lo! the jubilant sweet note tells
The wonder of His Easter bells.

Mixed hardwood forest, Warren, New Hampshire.
Photograph by William H. Johnson

A Sunrise Service

Pamela Kennedy

One of the advantages of marriage to a military man is the opportunity to move from place to place. In twenty-six years of Navy life together, we have moved seventeen times and enjoyed the customs and scenery of many different locales. We've spent Christmas in the snowy northeastern United States as well as in the desert climate of the Southwest. We've enjoyed Thanksgiving feasts near Plymouth Rock and at a Hawaiian beach made of lava from a still-active volcano. But one of the most unusual holiday celebrations I've experienced was an Easter sunrise service conducted on the flight deck of the USS *Essex*, a helicopter carrier passing through Pearl Harbor on its way back to San Diego, California.

It seemed an unlikely place to celebrate the Resurrection, a scene I always associate with a quiet garden shrouded in early morning mist. As we walked along the pier where the *Essex* was moored, I heard the rumble and whir of engines, the creak of taut lines straining. I was dwarfed by the huge superstructure as deck after deck of battle gray towered above us. We climbed two flights of metal stairs (*ladders* in Navy jargon) and crossed the ramp bridging the space between pier and ship. Serious young men in crisp, white uni-

Photograph by Tim Fitzharris/Minden Pictures

forms greeted us with salutes and welcomed us aboard. As a small group gathered on the quarter-deck, an escort came to lead us to the flight deck for the services. We wound our way like obedient sheep through mazes of equipment, passageways, ladders, and ramps until we eventually emerged on the flight deck—a vast gray platform at the stern of the ship. On one side of the deck a half dozen battle-ready helicopters were lashed down with inch-thick cables, a menacing venue in which to celebrate the bright hope of Easter morning.

Above us, dark, threatening clouds piled upon one another. The wind whipped across the deck ferociously, knocking over carefully placed Easter lilies, music stands, and metal folding chairs; tearing at flags and skirts and pant legs. A balding Marine sergeant fiddled with a tape recorder, connecting and disconnecting wires, turning dials, inserting and ejecting cassettes. What a scene! I wondered who had decided this would be a good idea. Then I felt a few drops of rain. How could anyone be expected to worship under such conditions?

The static crackle of electricity through the amplifier signaled the sergeant had apparently made the right connections. After a few more pops and screeches, his deep voice interrupted my troubled meditation on wind and rain and quiet Easters past. He welcomed us to the *Essex*, then began to sing in a rich baritone that wrapped itself around the deck in the dark morning. His words reminded us of the solemn march of Mary Magdalene on Easter morning, of her despair and fears, her misunderstandings, her grief. I looked up at the gloomy clouds towering over the maintains and wondered about Mary's doubts that must have piled one upon the other. Then the key changed, and he sang of the unexpected joy she found at the feet of her resurrected Lord as He spoke her name and she realized new hope. There was a murmur in the small congregation gathered on the flight deck, and a little girl pointed to the eastern sky. Thick and golden against the shades of black and gray, wide swaths of sunlight radiated from the broken clouds, falling on the mountains and the wind-whipped water of the harbor. Whitecaps flashed in the streaming light, and we all sat motionless, hushed by the scene before us.

After a few moments, I looked around the flight deck again. We sat on the deck of one of the Navy's most powerful vessels, surrounded by monuments to military technology, yet we were speechless before the magnificence of God's creation. The men and women in this congregation had dedicated themselves to fight their country's battles using all the weapons at their disposal, yet the morning's display of natural beauty said more about the triumph of light over darkness, of good over evil than all the warships and planes humans would ever create. I realized that Easter was not so much about peace and quiet as it was about war. Somehow this ship now seemed a perfect place to recall that the ultimate battle of life and death was not fought in a dewy garden, but in the dirt and dust of the everyday world. And it was also a perfect place to remember that we need not fear defeat, for the victory has already been secured by our heavenly Captain.

The Garden of Gethsemane, Israel. Photograph by R. Kord/Robertstock

Jesus in the Garden
Luke 22:39–48

And he came out, and went, as he was wont, to the mount of Olives; and his disciples also followed him.

And when he was at the place, he said unto them, Pray that ye enter not into temptation.

And he was withdrawn from them about a stone's cast, and kneeled down, and prayed,

Saying, Father, if thou be willing, remove this cup from me: nevertheless not my will, but thine, be done.

And there appeared an angel unto him from heaven, strengthening him. And being in an agony he prayed more earnestly . . .

And when he rose up from prayer, and was come to his disciples, he found them sleeping for sorrow, And said unto them, Why sleep ye? rise and pray, lest ye enter into temptation.

And while he yet spake, behold a multitude, and he that was called Judas, one of the twelve, went before them, and drew near unto Jesus to kiss him.

Jesus said unto him, Judas, betrayest thou the Son of man with a kiss?

They Crucified Him

Luke 23:33–34a, 44–47, 49

And when they were come to the place, which is called Calvary, there they crucified him, and the malefactors, one on the right hand, and the other on the left. Then said Jesus, Father, forgive them; for they know not what they do. . . .

And it was about the sixth hour, and there was a darkness over all the earth until the ninth hour. And the sun was darkened, and the veil of the temple was rent in the midst.

And when Jesus had cried with a loud voice, he said, Father, into thy hands I commend my spirit: and having said thus, he gave up the ghost.

Now when the centurion saw what was done, he glorified God, saying, Certainly this was a righteous man. . . .

And all his acquaintance, and the women that followed him from Galilee, stood afar off, beholding these things.

Via Dolorosa, Jerusalem, Israel. Photograph by R. Kord/Robertstock

Tomb in Jerusalem, Israel. Photograph by Brand X/SuperStock

Easter Sunday
John 20:1–16

The first day of the week cometh Mary Magdalene early, when it was yet dark, unto the sepulchre, and seeth the stone taken away from the sepulchre.

Then she runneth, and cometh to Simon Peter, and to the other disciple, whom Jesus loved, and saith unto them, They have taken away the Lord out of the sepulchre, and we know not where they have laid him.

Peter therefore went forth, and that other disciple, and came to the sepulchre. So they ran both together: and the other disciple did outrun Peter, and came first to the sepulchre. And he stooping down, and looking in, saw the linen clothes lying; yet went he not in.

Then cometh Simon Peter following him, and went into the sepulchre, and seeth the linen clothes lie, And the napkin that was about his head, not lying with the linen clothes, but wrapped together in a place by itself. . . . Then the disciples went away again unto their own home.

But Mary stood without at the sepulchre weeping: and as she wept, she stooped down, and looked into the sepulchre, And seeth two angels in white sitting, the one at the head, and the other at the feet, where the body of Jesus had lain.

And they say unto her, Woman, why weepest thou? She saith unto them, Because they have taken away my Lord, and I know not where they have laid him. And when she had thus said, she turned herself back, and saw Jesus standing, and knew not that it was Jesus.

Jesus saith unto her, Woman, why weepest thou? whom seekest thou?

She, supposing him to be the gardener, saith unto him, Sir, if thou have borne him hence, tell me where thou hast laid him, and I will take him away.

Jesus saith unto her, Mary.

She turned herself, and saith unto him, Rabboni; which is to say Master.

Jesus Appears
on the Shore
John 21:2–17

There were together Simon Peter, and Thomas called Didymus, and Nathanael of Cana in Galilee, and the sons of Zebedee, and two other of his disciples.

Simon Peter saith unto them, I go a fishing. They say unto him, We also go with thee. They went forth, and entered into a ship immediately; and that night they caught nothing.

But when the morning was now come, Jesus stood on the shore: but the disciples knew not that it was Jesus.

Then Jesus saith unto them, Children, have ye any meat? They answered him, No.

And he said unto them, Cast the net on the right side of the ship, and ye shall find. They cast therefore, and now they were not able to draw it for the multitude of fishes.

Therefore that disciple whom Jesus loved saith unto Peter, It is the Lord. . . .

And the other disciples came in a little ship; (for they were not far from land, but as it were two hundred cubits,) dragging the net with fishes.

As soon then as they were come to land, they saw a fire of coals there, and fish laid thereon, and bread.

Jesus saith unto them, Bring of the fish which ye have now caught.

Simon Peter went up, and drew the net to land full of great fishes, an hundred and fifty and three: and for all there were so many, yet was not the net broken.

Jesus saith unto them, Come and dine. And none of the disciples durst ask him, Who art thou? knowing that it was the Lord.

Jesus then cometh, and taketh bread, and giveth them, and fish likewise.

This is now the third time that Jesus shewed himself to his disciples, after that he was risen from the dead.

Sea of Galilee. Photograph by Jon Arnold Images/SuperStock

Sunrise
George L. Ehrman

Very early in the morning
At the rising of the sun,
They came and saw the stone
        was rolled away.
An angel in the sepulchre
Spoke to each and every one,
"Behold the place where once
your Savior lay."

They went out from
        the place of night
Into a garden filled with light
And found our Savior there.

They found Him on a lonely road,
They found Him where
        each one abode,
For He was everywhere!

Very early here this morning
At the rising of the sun,
We come because the stone
        was rolled away.
Each a bearer of glad tidings,
Witnessing to everyone,
"He lives within my heart
        this Easter Day!"

For This Day
Peter Marshall

We thank Thee for the beauty of this day, for the glorious message that all nature proclaims: the Easter lilies with their waxen throats eloquently singing the good news; the birds, so early this morning, impatient to begin their song; every flowering tree, shrub, and flaming bush, a living proclamation from Thee. Oh, open our hearts that we may hear it too!

Lead us, we pray Thee, to the grave that is empty, into the garden of the Resurrection where we may meet our risen Lord. May we never again live as if Thou were dead!

In Thy presence restore our faith, our hope, our joy. Grant to our spirits refreshment, rest, and peace. Maintain within our hearts an unruffled calm, an unbroken serenity that no storms of life shall ever be able to take from us. From this moment, O living Christ, we ask Thee to go with us wherever we go; be our Companion in all that we do. And for this greatest of all gifts, we offer Thee our sacrifices of thanksgiving. Amen.

Oak branch in fog. Photograph by Peter Gerdehag/Briljans/Jupiter Images

Faith

John Richard Moreland

In every leaf that crowns the plain,
In every violet 'neath the hill,
In every yellow daffodil
I see the risen Lord again.

In each arbutus flower I see
A faith that lived through frost and snow,
And in the birds that northward go,
A guiding hand's revealed to me.

Lo! winter from some dark abyss
Came forth to kill all growing things;
'Twas vain; spring rose on emerald wings,
Moth-like from her dead chrysalis.

Each germ within the tiny seed
Throws off the husk that to it clings,
And toward the sun it upward brings
New life to blossom to its need.

Ye hearts that mourn, rise up and sing!
Death has no power to hold its prey,
The grave is only where we lay
The soul for its eternal spring!

In every leaf that crowns the plain,
In every violet 'neath the hill,
In every yellow daffodil
I see the risen Lord again.

ISBN-13: 978-0-8249-1313-7
ISBN-10: 0-8249-1313-2

Published by Ideals Publications, a Guideposts Company
535 Metroplex Drive, Suite 250, Nashville, Tennessee 37211
www.idealspublications.com

Editor, Melinda Rathjen
Art Director, Marisa Jackson
Permissions, Patsy Jay
Copy Editor, Kaye Dacus

Cover photograph: Frost on crocuses. Photograph by Fred Habegger/
    Grant Heilman Photography, Inc.
Inside front cover: Painting by George Hinke
Inside back cover: Painting by George Hinke

ACKNOWLEDGMENTS

BORLAND, HAL. "Beyond" from *Sundial of the Seasons* by Hal Borland. Copyright © 1964 by Hal Borland, Renewed © 1992 by Donal Borland. Used by permission of Frances Collin. FLOYD, BLANCHE. "Plum Silk Dress." Reprinted by permission from *Good Old Days Specials* magazine and *Bringing in the Sheaves*, edited by Ken and Janice Tate, published by DRG, Berne, IN 46711. HUGHES, LANGSTON. "In Time of Silver Rain" from *Collected Poems by Langston Hughes*, Copyright © 1994 by the Estate of Langston Hughes. Published by Alfred A. Knopf, Random House. KRONSCHNABEL, DARLENE. "A Country-Style Easter" from *Seasons In a Country Kitchen*. Copyright © 2005 by author Darlene Kronschnabel. Published by Jones Books. MARSHALL, PETER. "For This Day." From *The Prayers of Peter Marshall*, Copyright © 1982 by Catherine Marshall. Published by Baker Book House Company. MOOTH, VERLA. "An Easter To Remember." Reprinted by permission from *Good Old Days Specials* magazine and *Bringing in the Sheaves*, edited by Ken and Janice Tate, published by DRG, Berne, IN 46711.

Our sincere thanks to the following authors or their heirs, for material submitted to *Ideals* for publication: George L. Ehrman, Hilda Butler Farr, Loise Pinkerton Fritz, Frances Mary Frost, Earle J. Grant, Lola M. Hazard, Pamela Kennedy, Lona Pearson McDorman, Esta McElrath, Mamie Ozburn Odum, Catherine Otten, Wanda M. Read, Shirley Sallay, Ruth Powell Singer, Jan Stephens, Rachel Van Creme, Grace V. Watkins, May Smith White, Kathryn Stephenson Wilhelm, and Isabelle Carter Young. Every effort has been made to establish ownership and use of each selection in this book. If contacted, the publisher will be pleased to rectify any inadvertent errors or omissions in subsequent reprints.